Sunday, January 18, 2015

Revisiting Stigma:

The Game of Appearances

I0445878

A Sociological Perspective

Doesn't the term stigma harken us back to Sociology 101? Those were the days when Irving Goffman was in the spotlight. Goffman got famous from his work on stigma and the social forces that shape our identity. What made him special was his ability to capture human experience, which made him a psychologist/sociologist of sorts. Despite its far-reaching implications and relevance, the phenomenon of stigma seems to have dropped off of the map of required knowledge for those in the helping professions. Becoming conscious of and understanding our relationship with society, and how this relationship effects how we feel about ourselves and how we act in our relationships, can have transformative potential. It can empower us to made decisions and behave is a way that is consistent with our purpose.

A stigma is a visible or known attribute that relegates a person to a sub-standard or less desirable category of people. When a person is stigmatized, our perceptions and treatment towards that person are affected. The person gets labeled as "defective," and subsequently branded as an outcast, an example of what not to be. The person's status – how s/he is seen in the eyes of others, and how s/he will

1

ultimately feel about him/herself, are all under arbitrary and brutal assault. Whether aware or not, the tendency is to react with avoidance, indifference and disdain.

The kind of deep silent pain that a stigmatized person suffers when one knows that what s/he is at his/her core is unwanted, unworthy and not belonging can break a person. Stigma causes shame and alienation to pervade one's sense of self and relationships.

Stigmatization

Stigmatization is a process of societal and familial conditioning. By the time we're adults, the negative reactions and judgments associated to any stigmatized condition are deeply ingrained in our consciousness. Those who carry a stigma know that they will be discredited the moment their stigma becomes known. One can expect a desperate effort to escape rejection by keeping any potential stigma hidden. When the condition is visible, there is no way to hide it; one must learn to live with the stigma.

The difference in perception between a visible stigmatized condition, such as obesity, and an invisible one such as an addiction or being gay, is extremely significant. When the condition is invisible, appearance and deception come into play to keep it invisible. "A solution for the individual who can't maintain an identity norm is to alienate him/herself from the community, which upholds the norm, or refrain from developing an attachment to the community." (Goffman)

The phenomenon of stigmatization is born out of the political and social power structure that sets the standard for acceptability, worthiness and normalcy. The contingencies determining what is considered desirable are decided and transmitted by those in power. In any society, there are those who do the discrediting and those who are discredited. Stigma is the weapon used to restore the norm for the

entire social system, enforcing conformity by arbitrarily punishing
those who deviate from those standards, regardless of how unrealistic
those standards may be.

The powers that be in the socio-political hierarchy get to define
desirability and undesirability, which is everything you want and
don't want to be. Desirability is the reward for those who appear
"together," in control, invulnerable and exude pleasantness all of the
time. The rewards of fame, adoration, wealth, prestige, and power are
certainly tantalizing inducements. Undesirability is the punishment
for not being able to appear "together". It is also the punishment for
those who are seen as having problems, expressing pain and who
need help.

Regardless of the reasons or circumstances, a person unable to
conform to the standards society deems normal gets stigmatized. The
person is disgraced, treated as weak, evil, immoral, incapable and
unworthy. S/he is reduced from a whole and usual person to a tainted
and discounted one. "The standards s/he has incorporated from the
wider society cause him/her to agree that s/he does indeed fall short
of what s/he ought to be. Shame becomes a central possibility, arising
from the individual's perception of one's own attributes as defiling to
possess." (Goffman)

A person unable to conform is considered to be different and will be
stigmatized for being different. Not only are we conditioned to have
our acts together, when encountering someone or something that taps
our awareness of the condition to the fore, our defense system adapts
accordingly. Denial keeps the shame, fear and helplessness from our
conscious minds.

Being "nice" can lead to pity...

When considering that being "nice" is akin to conforming; that is,
there is a stigma associated with not being 'nice,' we can begin to

3

Daniel Linder MA, MFT
Daniel@RelationshipVision.com

appreciate how incredibly subtle and layered the effects of stigma are. Given that contempt, rejection or simply seeing someone in a less favorable light may not fit with a 'nice' persona, we'll act in a way that is more consistent with being nice. Rather than acknowledging our contempt, we might instead act as if we care, for caring is the "right" thing to do, but which will ultimately come across as pity. Pity only further degrades the stigmatized person, and perpetuates the game of appearances.

While pity may sound and look like caring, it is not real caring, and has different affects. When pity is expressed, the interaction is filtered through an artificial screen, unacknowledged emotional distance is maintained. The non-verbal, and sometimes verbal messages are, "Too bad this had to happen." "Too bad you're an addict." Implied in these messages is that, "We're different. I am well and you are sick. I'm okay, and you're not. You have worse problems than I do."

We are just touching upon the enormity to stigma's rippling effect. Not only are we conditioned to make things appear better than they actually are, we are also conditioned to deceive others and ourselves.

The rippling effects of stigma go as far as distorting our notion of willpower and what is means to be human. We'll tend to not realize the limitations of our willpower until we are forced to, i.e. as in the case of later stage addiction, when one is "bottoming out." Surrendering to these realizations, i.e. not being able to control an addiction, solve the problem, make the pain go away, can become bitterly disillusioning, shame-inducing experiences.

The same process plays out in our relationships. What often happens is that we get stuck on how we want to see each other, as opposed to seeing each other more objectively or realistically. We prefer to see each other in a more desirable or idealized light than is actually the case. We're anti objectivity, anti reality, ego-driven. We'll inflate positive qualities while deflating negative ones; limitations, flaws, problems, issues, even mistakes, to always maintain a favorable picture, the one we wish to paint. If effect, we're blinding ourselves in the service of our egos.

Seeing each other in real, as opposed to ideal, terms becomes a highly risky situation, especially when considering that there is a stigma attached to seeing each other realistically, when it means falling short of an ideal or of what one wants to believe. This obviously poses an obstacle in achieving and sustaining intimacy. Getting to know and understand each other, let alone, deeply, become impossible when the name of the game is one of appearances; when we're conditioned to present and see preferred versions of ourselves, rather than "warts and all" versions. Collusion is involved, a conspiracy against seeing the truth about who we are as human beings.

Case Example

In the session from which the following excerpt is taken, Sam (patient) sees through his own act and the lengths he'd gone to present a certain façade, the "games" (as he referred to them) he played for desirability. He talks about where and how he learned to play these games, how he really felt inside and how difficult it is to not play them.

At the time of this dialogue, Sam had returned to treatment after a one year absence and having maintained sobriety for a year.

Sam (S)   I didn't want to come today. I've been doing real well. My day was going fine until an hour or so ago and I'm thinking, "I don't need this." I feel so uncomfortable. Why am I doing this to myself?

Daniel(D)   Why did you come in?

S   It was when I ran into you at the supermarket.

D   That was quite a while ago.

S   I told you that I wanted to return only because I thought I should. I said what I thought you wanted to hear.

D   Say what I wanted to hear?

S   Yeah. Like when you ask me how I'm doing, I say want to come back cause that's what I'm supposed to say.

D   Are you saying that you called me to fulfill a lie?

S   If I didn't call, I'd look bad.

D   How you appear is a primary motivation… You look you have more to say.

S   One of the main fears I have about coming here is that I'm going to have that blank look on my face and I won't know what to do, or say. I hate that look. A part of me wants to be a good client and be more comfortable talking about myself.

D   You put a lot of pressure on yourself.

|S   I'm always trying to impress everyone. I want to be up there with the good guys.

D   What are you aware of right now?

S   Tension. Anxiety.

D   That happens when you feel that you must hide what you really feel inside.

S   I always make things up. At work, I always say that I made more sales than I really did. Stuff to look good. Stupid games. Stupid lies are what they are. It's a habit. (pause) I'm really nervous. My hands are wet with sweat…I've got that blank look on my face, don't I?

D   You must feel quite awkward when you're not busy impressing people.

S   I don't know what is supposed to happen here.

D   Especially when you're unsure how to impress me. If only you knew how to be a good client… How long have you been trying to impress people?

S   It started with my parents. I know that.

D   They encouraged you to present a more together front.

S   I always made sure I got good grades.

D   You got stroked for being a "good" boy, while you kept other parts of yourself hidden.

S   (blank expression)

D   You have that blank look on your face.

S   I drifted off.

D   What's the last thing you remember me saying?

S   I can't remember.

      Copyrighted Materials 2007
Daniel@RelationshipVision.com

D	I was saying that the better you played the game, the more praise you got, but the worse you felt.
S	I remember they (parents) always saying that I was better and smarter than my friends.
D	Do you remember you that made you feel?
S	I lied. I made up stuff about them, trying to get my parents to like them more… I don't know whether I want to open a can of worms.
D	My sense is that you feel insecure when you aren't hiding behind your game. Not playing is unfamiliar, overwhelming.
S	There are days when I get up in the morning and pray that I get through the day without doing it. And before I know it, I'm doing it.
D	Like the game is running you.
S	It scares me.

      Copyrighted Materials 2007
Daniel@RelationshipVision.com

The process of therapy was paradoxical for Sam. When the light got turned on and he saw through his "game, he got terrified. The closer he got to real feelings, the more insecure and lost he felt, like he was a fish out of water. He was more "at home" in a defense mode than when feeling his feelings. Therapy was like a roller coaster ride, approaching, then avoiding feelings.

Sam is probably one of many who live their lives dreading this "ultimate" confrontation, facing their real feelings. All the while, they're living jaded existences, banking on the illusion of normalcy and desirability. All the while, thinking, "Not know. Later. I'll deal with it tomorrow" as if they could borrow time and postpone indefinitely the end of their game.

Where There is Stigma, There is Internalized Shame

In his book, <u>Shame, The Power of Caring</u>, Gershen Kaufman focuses on the experience of shame. He contends that shame is the most unbearable feeling known to humankind. That shame can contaminate a person's whole identity and how one feels about oneself. Shame becomes internalized. The number and intensity of shame inducing experiences determines the extent to which personality develops as a defense against the feeling of shame. Self-talk and belief systems are variations on the same theme: self-degradation. "I'm a failure." I'm a loser." "I'm not good enough." "I'm not lovable." "The moment I open up and let myself be known, it's the end of the relationship. The person will surely leave. Kaufman's work attests to the power of stigma, it's potential to dictate how we act in our relationships, because stigma induces shame.

In the case of addiction and other invisible conditions, stigmatization takes effect the moment the condition becomes known. The depth of pain and shame associated with stigma require the development of psychological defenses that counteract it. The huge stigma that addiction still carries (despite being deemed a disease) acts as a powerful incentive that bolsters the addict's defense system. And, it is not just the addict we're talking about, it is the significant others and everyone else involved who relies on denial. As long as s/he doesn't expose his/her addiction to anyone, let alone, realize there is a problem, s/he'll remain insulated from the intense shame and alienation that would otherwise be triggered.

Night, Mother: Stigma and Suicide

Excerpts of dialogue taken from the play, Night, Mother by Marsha Norman serve as dramatic examples of how the stigma attached to a disease (epilepsy) affects the relationships and communication within a family. The story revolves around a mother's efforts to stop her daughter from committing suicide. The last scene is the sound of a gun shot.

Mama (M)   I think your daddy had fits, too. I think he sat in His chair and had little fits. I read this a long time ago in a magazine, how little fits go, just little blackouts where maybe their eyes don't even close and people just call them "thinking spells."

The magazine said that some people don't even know they've had one.

Jessie (J)   Daddy would have known if he had fits, Mama.

M   Jessie, listen to what I'm telling you. This lady had anywhere between five and five hundred fits a day and they lasted maybe fifteen seconds a piece, so that out her life, she'd only lost two weeks altogether.

J   You want to talk about fits, is that it?

Daniel@RelationshipVision.com

It's apparent in the above dialogue that Mama's display of ignorance -- referring to seizures as fits only further perpetuated that stigma attached to the disease of epilepsy. The stigma is directly related to the convulsions or seizures that can be frequent occurrences, and which can also be unwholesome, sometimes frightening sights. Epileptic seizures became known as "fits," which are sudden, violent access of some specified emotion," synonymous with "tantrums." Referring to them as fits implied a mental and emotional imbalance, which carries an even greater stigma than an epileptic seizure, convulsion or neurological disorder. When seizures became known as fits, a derogatory term is used in daily discourse as a source of metaphor and imagery without giving thought to the original meaning, and a wide range of imperfections was imputed to the original one. (Goffman)

It's also apparent that Mama was also trying to minimize the fact that Jessie was subjected to seizures, which obviously added weight to the burden of shame Jessie had already internalized. While Mama was clearly trying to make Jessie feel better, she was clearly failing miserably. First she suggests that you're barely aware that anything is awry by referring to them as "thinking spells." Again she tries to minimize them by implying that they are so frequent, yet short-lasting, they're incidental and hardly matter. Mama was inadvertently making a bad situation worse, bringing more attention to the stigma in her effort to deny it.

The next section captures horrific images conjured up and consistent with how one of Jesse's seizures were seen through the eyes of another, her mother.

J   Most of the time I wouldn't know I'd had one, except when I wake up in the morning with different clothes on, feeling like I'd been run over.

M   I can tell when you're about to have one. Your eyes get this big!

J   (Taking charge of this) What do they look like, the seizures?

M   (Reluctant) Different each time, Jess.

J   O.K. Pick one, then. A good one. I think I want to know now.

M   There's not much to tell. You just…crumble, in a heap, like a puppet and somebody cut the strings all at once, or like the firing squad in some Mexican movie, you just slide down the wall you know. You don't know what happens? How could you not know what happens?

J   I'm busy.

M   That's not funny.

J   I'm not laughing. My head turns around and I fall down and then what?

M   Well, your chest squeezes in and out, and you sound like you're gagging, sucking air in and out like you can't breathe.

J   Do it for me. Make the sound for me.

M   I will not. It's awful sounding.

J   Yeah. What's next?

M   Your mouth bites down and I have to get your tongue out of the way fast, so you don't bite yourself.

J   Or you. I bite you, too, don't I?

M   You got me once real good. I had to get a tetanus shot. And then you start to turn blue and the jerks start up.

J   Foaming like a mad dog the whole time.

M   It's bubbling, Jess, not foam like the washer overflowed, or, for god's sake it's bubbling like a baby spitting up. I go to get a wet washcloth, that's all. And the jerks slow down and you wet yourself and its over. Two minutes tops.

J   How do I get to bed?

M   How do you think?

J   I'm too heavy for you now. How do you do it?

M   I call Dawson. But I get you cleaned up before he gets here and I make him leave before you get up.

J   You could just leave me on the floor.

M   I want you to wake up some place nice, O.K?

We see that Jesse establishes that she is well aware of the truth, the horrible truth. She gets her mother to describe the unspeakable. Mama is temporarily freed up from the shackles of denial, able to provide graphic details. However, we can see that she is still trying to protect Jesse by making the fits sound entertaining, like cartoons, which have

Copyrighted Materials 2007
Daniel@RelationshipVision.com
the effect of bringing more attention to something being wrong or shameful about Jesse's condition.

When Mama depicts herself as attentive by going to such great lengths in her care taking of Jesse, we can see that she is inadvertently perpetuating the secret. And in so doing, Jesse confirms for herself. That she was always treated as if there was indeed something inherently shameful about her fits, as they had to be kept secret.

In the following scene, Mama is trying to convince Jesse that there is reason to live. But ironically, her explanation for Jesse's fits and accounting for how she handled her having epilepsy seals Jesse's fate. Suffice it to say that Mama's efforts to avert Jesse's suicide were unsuccessful. It becomes clearly apparent that Mama's misrepresentation and outright deception served to further reinforce internalized shame and alienation that begun when Jesse was a child.

M   The fits are over!

J   It's not the fits, Mama.

M   Then it's me for giving them to you, but I didn't do it! Your daddy gave you those fits, Jesse. He passed them down to you like your green eyes and your straight hair. It's not my fault!

J   So what if he had little fits? It's not inherited. I fell off of a horse. It was an accident.

M   The horse wasn't the first time, Jesse. You had a fit when you were five years old.

J   I did not.

M   You were eating a popsicle and down you went. He gave it to you. It's his fault, not mine.

Daniel@RelationshipVision.com

J   Well, you took your time telling me.

M   How do you tell that to a five year old?

J   What did the doctor say?

M   He said kid have them all of the time. He said there wasn't anything to do but wait for another one.

J   But I didn't have another one… You mean to tell me I had fits all the time as a kid and you told me I fell down or something and it wasn't until I had the fit when Cecil was looking that anyone bothered to find out what was wrong with me?

M   It wasn't **all the time**, Jesse. They changed when you started school.

J   How many fits did I have?

M   You never hurt yourself. I never let you out of my sight. I caught you every time.

J   But you tell anybody.

M   It was none of their business.

J   You were ashamed.

M   I didn't want anyone to know, least of all you.

J   Least of all me. Oh right, that was mine to know Mama, not yours. Did Daddy know?

M   He thought… you fell down a lot. That's what he thought. You were careless. Or maybe he thought I beat you. I don't know what he thought. He didn't think about it.

J   Because you didn't tell him.

M   If I told him about you, I'd have to tell him about him.

J   I don't like this. I don't like this one bit.

M   I didn't think you'd like this. That's why I didn't tell you.
J   If he knew I was epileptic, Mama, I wouldn't have ridden any horses.

M   Make you feel like a freak, is that what I should have done? Maybe I did drop you, you don't know. Maybe I fed you the wrong thing. Maybe you had a fever some time and I didn't know soon enough. Maybe it's a punishment.

J   For what?

M   I don't know. Because of how I felt about your father. Because I didn't want anymore children. Because I smoked too much or didn't eat right when I was carrying you. It had to be something I did.

J   It does not. It's just a sickness, not a curse. Epilepsy doesn't mean anything. It just is.

It seemed that everything Mama had said to explain her actions only exacerbated the situation and confirmed all of Jesse's suspicions. First she blames Jesse's father, as if he was responsible, and not her, for the horrible crime of causing Jesse's epilepsy. Then we become privy to the cause Jesse's confusion about whether or not epilepsy is inherited as she was lied to all along, having been told that it was the result of an accident, i.e. falling off of a horse. Mama defended herself by telling Jesse that she was too young to understand.

When Mama admits to having deliberately concealed that information from Jesse since age 5, she makes matters worse by revealing that she never bothered to find out what the problem was, never consulting with a doctor for a diagnosis until Cecil witnessed a seizure. In fact, Mama reveals that she never told anyone, "It was no one's business."

What would it have meant if someone found out Jesse had epilepsy? Mama saw herself as loyal and protective for having concealed the problem, "Make you feel like a freak. Is that what I should have done?" The most telling implication in Mama's portrayal of herself as an ally was going as far as hiding the existence of the disorder from her husband, Jesse's father, for he, too, was epileptic. In her mind, she was protecting him from the onslaught of shame that would have come crashing down on him the moment the stigmatized condition was exposed. Mama's need to keep the stigma secret took precedence over what her father knew or thought about his daughter's well-being. No matter whether he thought Jesse's "falling down a lot" was due to poor parenting, even abuse would have been easier to deal with than epilepsy. Mama went as far as risking Jesse's safety by allowing her to ride horses rather than letting anyone find out, including Jesse.

As a result of Mama's aversion to pursuing this matter further and accounting for Jesse's strange, "undesirable|" behavior by seeking professional consultation, no one in her family ever found out what was actually wrong; that her seizures were due to a neurological disorder called epilepsy, and that epilepsy is treatable!

Mama was operating as if she could protect her family from their own humanness. Her dogged persistence attests to the extent to which the stigma and associated shame were, both internalized and intolerable. Furthermore, it becomes apparent that she felt responsible for Jesse's epilepsy, that she must have fallen short in some way and which caused it. It appears that she never understands that epilepsy "just is." This was probably one of her limitations for she was a product of the familial and social conditioning of her time. She was taught to crucify herself for being vulnerable to one of nature's aberrations (epilepsy), one she didn't choose or could will away.

Despite her loneliness and desperation, Jesse was still able to articulate that epilepsy "just is," that a disease is a sickness, not a curse. Whether you judge it, wish it away, try to hide it, attribute it to other causes, or feel ashamed, it is what it is, a disease.

The Stigma of Addiction

Like epilepsy, addiction just is. Yet the effects of stigma are still prevail. Shame and secrecy govern every addicted family system, and are barriers the addict and all significant others must confront and overcome in order to heal. Granted, no one wants to have a disease. No one wants to admit to having a disease. But the point is what happens when you have a disease. Recognition and admission are pre-requisites to getting the necessary help or treatment. Stigma makes compassion towards oneself and each other a huge hurdle, accepting one's humanness out of reach.

Those who don't understand that a disease "just is," will likely consult with others who tell them that everything is okay, just as Mama did with the doctor who assured her that "kids have them all of the time." Without being aware, we have a way of relaying the message, "Please tell me there is nothing wrong." Most people are inclined to oblige, inadvertently willing to distort the facts so to not blemish a prettier picture.

Claudia Black, the acclaimed authority on Adult Children of Alcoholics, wrote in her book, It Could Never Happen to Me, discusses the 'Don't Talk' rule that all members in an alcoholic family abides by and that comes from the stigma attached to alcoholism. She uses the example of a young child asking his/her mother, "What's wrong with daddy?" when he is lying on the couch in a near comatose state from alcohol intoxication. And, mother answers matter of factly, "Daddy is sleeping," as if s/he was observing nothing out of the ordinary and there was no reason to be concerned. This misrepresentation, she explains, is at the bare minimum confusing for the child as it invalidates his/her concern. The children in such a system are trained to pretend that what they see is not what they see, but is something else. They get trained to think and communicate falsely. Yet, the undercurrent of shame, concern and confusion remains as they can't help but notice the incongruity. They intuitively put one and one together and get the message that no one is supposed to know; not just that Daddy was drinking, that he "sleeps a lot," has a problem or disease, and needs help. They never really find out the truth because it remains concealed from them; they know something is wrong, but don't know what the problem actually is.

Clinical Issues and Counter-transference

The influence of stigma and depth of shame can be and often is underestimated by treatment practitioners. This is especially relevant considering the variety of related clinical issues; those being preparedness for dealing with the many layers of stigma-based shame triggered when a stigmatized condition is identified, as in the case of addiction for example – beginning with having problems, being an addict, needing help, not having adequate will power, and for the hurt caused to oneself and others; all of which are major hurdles throughout recovery.

For example, a patient who had three years of sobriety reportedly felt pangs of remorse or shame when a friend offered him a "toke" on a joint and he declined the offer. Any environment or group atmosphere where recreational using is 'desirable' has the potential to trigger shame, regardless of how long the recovering person has maintained

Daniel@RelationshipVision.com

sobriety. Feeling good or shame-free remaining abstinent can only occur in a stigma-free situation, i.e. being with other sober people and when sobriety is the norm.

Homophobia and Intimacy

The following is my own story of revelation and transformation gained from my self-analysis and willingness to be honest with myself. While I was going through the process, it felt painfully difficult because I wanted to see myself as not being homophobic. But the experience made real a powerful lesson learned: Homophobia comes at the expense of intimacy, intimacy in both professional and personal contexts.

I'm Daniel. I'm heterosexual and (was) homophobic.

I can recall my high school days when gays were "fags," "pussies," "dykes," freaks, outsiders, non-entities, people you'd always get support for abusing, the safest of scapegoats. I wondered why I (and others) invariably reacted with avoidance, indifference and disdain., whether we were aware of it or not. I didn't understand how I was different or better. Certainly, I wasn't a pillar of normalcy, yet I was obviously better off than they were.

It wasn't until I was a freshman in college that I learned about stigma in a sociology class. A stigma is a visible or known attribute that relegates a person to a substandard or less desirable category of people. This person is disgraced, treated as weak, evil, immoral, defective, incapable and unworthy. But at the time, I hadn't made the connection that gay people were stigmatized, probably because "out of sight" meant "out of mind" to me.

        Copyrighted Materials 2007
Daniel@RelationshipVision.com

It wasn't until graduate school that I realized I was homophobic. It was there I first heard the term. My understanding was that it had to do with the stigma attached to being gay, an aversion to same gender sex accompanied by a devaluation of the person.

My homophobia was evident in the ways I reacted to the **idea** of men having sex with other men, women having sex with other women; of a man wanting to have sex with me and of me having sex with a man. I was aware of an ingrained, almost automatic fear and revulsion, and was able to talk about it. More alarming, however, were its unconscious manifestations – how my homophobia influenced my behavior whenever I was with someone who was gay. I acted respectfully and even honestly. I was able to laugh with the person, ask for help and offer help. I knew how to be nice. But then, after we parted, it seemed I was relieved.

As I developed more understanding of my homophobia and homophobia in general, I saw there was a distinction between **blatant** and **sophisticated** homophobia. When it's blatant, homophobia usually comes across as ignorance or malevolence. When it's sophisticated, the person's attitude is more subtle; pretension, concealment and denial are involved.

The question I eventually had to ask myself was how emotionally close can or would I allow myself to get to someone who is gay. Although I wanted to see myself as someone who treats every person as equal, I wasn't sure I was capable of doing so. Since my contact with the gay population was minimal, I hadn't explored this question much further.

Daniel@RelationshipVision.com

It was when I decided to get more involved professionally with the gay population that I was, once again, confronted by this question.

I was putting together my first gay men's **Dating to Relate** workshop, which was about developing dating and intimacy skills. Up to this point I had done only heterosexual groups and workshops.

One of the participants told me he had AIDS and wanted me to call the other group members to make sure his having AIDS was okay with them. I was under the impression that if someone is not actually sick, they probably don't have AIDS, they're merely HIV-positive. After I had spoken to the other group members, I let him know that none of them had a problem with his being HIV-positive. He later called back to tell me that my ignorance about HIV and AIDS made him feel unsafe being in a therapy group with me as the leader.

During the course of conversation, it became clear to me that I was not only dealing with someone who was gay, but someone with a disease, someone who could get sick and die. Suddenly I felt exposed and vulnerable. It dawned on me that I had kept myself insulated or emotionally removed from the reality of AIDS, despite all the attention it received in the media. Why was AIDS something that wasn't real to me until it was in my face? Was it my homophobia? Or did it have more to do with my aversion to disease and death? Either way I had to respond to him. He wanted my assurance that I understood his considerations and he responded with a decision to be in the group.

This conversation changed me. I got much closer to him than I had anticipated. I found myself getting intimately involved

Daniel@RelationshipVision.com

with a gay man who has AIDS and knew I was going to get even more involved with him during the group. I accepted the fact that I couldn't take his AIDS away from him, that he and AIDS were a package deal. In that moment, I also realized that his being gay was the same thing; it's impossible to totally accept someone who is gay without accepting his or her sexual orientation.

This was just the beginning of my metamorphosis.

During the workshop, it became apparent that, just like me, these gay men were also homophobic. But unlike me, their fear and revulsion were directed at themselves and profoundly affected their experience in relationships.

Not only was their homophobia an obstacle with which they had to contend, they had to overcome the kind of deep, silent pain that stigmatized people suffer when they know that what they are at their core is unwanted, unworthy and doesn't belong. Several of them discussed homophobia as a determining factor in their emotional and sexual development, and as an impediment in developing sexual and intimate relationships.

One of the group participants noted, "Growing up, being gay was the absolute worst thing in the world. It was the lowest low of human beings. Gay sex was what distinguished me from other people. It was taboo for me to express my sexuality. There were no role models around me. I didn't receive any positive messages. I didn't know any gay people. There were no gay people in my family. I had no gay friends. To me, gay sex was perverted, wrong, dirty and awful. The anonymous sex I had, which was about 95% of all the sex I had was a playing out of society's expectations of how I should have sex. And I did a remarkably good job. The only

options I had were furtive and shameful. Even after I came
out, this pattern was so ingrained in me it persisted, that all I
could have was that kind of sex and part of me still believes
that gay sex should be anonymous, that it belongs in
bathrooms or the park."

Someone else added, "And it's part of what made the gay
community such a fertile place for HIV to land. Our culture
doesn't support monogamous relationships between the same
sexes. It supports those kinds of encounters: bath houses,
parks, bookstores, gas stations, where we don't know our
partners. We don't like what you do, but if you're going to do
it, keep it in sleazy places where we don't have to see it or
know about it. If it were okay to make a commitment to
another person, anonymous sex wouldn't be as prevalent as it
is and nor would the gay population be such a hotbed for
sexually transmitted diseases."

As we discussed the issue of homophobia further, it became
apparent that homophobia isn't merely a part of our social
conditioning; it exists in our families as well, where it is
probably the most well-disguised. It was unanimously
accepted among the group members that being gay or living
a gay lifestyle was not an option for them. Whether the
messages were implicit or explicit, they felt being gay was a
source of embarrassment and disappointment to their
parents.

These men taught me a lot about something I'd had no
experience of, namely, what it's like to grow up in an
extremely homophobic society. At the same time, however,
I was deeply disturbed. I couldn't help but wonder, What if
most people are like how I used to be: uninformed, afraid
and judgmental? How many people really want to know
what it's like being gay? What it's like growing up in a

Daniel@RelationshipVision.com

culture that rejects and denies your very essence, what it's like to have parents who can't and in many cases never will accept you, what it's like to be different from everyone else, to live in secrecy, to be hated and mocked so long that you actually believe you are incapable if intimacy, and as a result, resort to anonymous sex as the only available means for sexual/human contact, yet are like everyone else, yearning for love?

Stigma poses potential counter-transference issues for the helping professional who underestimates or is unaware of its presence. Clinicians are human beings, not immune or impervious to stigma's far-reaching effects. Socially indoctrinated judgments can, and often do find their way into the clinician's head. For example, the professional might be unaware the s/he sees an addicted patient in a less desirable light, as opposed to someone in the throes of a disease. The counselor might not have any idea that his/her level of compassion is diminished and outlook dimmed. The counselor might look for other causes; miss the primary problems staring him/her in the face, and focus instead on secondary ones. If unaware, the tendency would be to shy away from the diagnosis of addiction so as not to have to deal with all of the uncomfortable ramifications.

While the idea here is for the clinician to work towards minimizing counter-transference by examining the impact of stigma on him/herself, doing so can pose an interesting dilemma. When the norm for therapists is to always strive for unconditional acceptance of the patient – not having any judgments—realizing one's own deep dark thoughts, i.e. one's homophobia runs counter to the ideal of being a good therapist, can become a shame inducing experience in its own right. By rejecting or denying one's judgments or other stigma-related reactions, the clinician is at risk of revealing the damaging judgments s/he is harboring, inadvertently

                              Copyrighted Materials 2007
Daniel@RelationshipVision.com

reinforcing the patient's shame by mirroring another human caught in the stranglehold of stigma. Additionally, if the issue of stigma is not adequately confronted and the counselor remains insulated from his/her own reactivity, s/he will not be tuned into his/her patient's emotional experience, let alone, level of internalized shame. It's absolutely necessary for the helping professional to be aware of the social climate, and reckon with the fact that s/he could be at the effect of the prevailing stigma-based norms, i.e. standards for desirability.

The clinician must understand that an addict is the stigma incarnate. Being addicted is 'undesirable,' representing everything one is not supposed to be. The addict can no longer adhere to the standard of desirability or play the game. S/he reflects back to the therapist only the starkest of visions of him/herself, one's s/he is not accustomed to or preferred. The more together the act, the easier it is to foster the illusion of competency, as opposed to exposing our humanity.

As the clinician becomes more aware of the powerful effects of stigma, s/he will be able to incorporate the disease concept into his/her work. The disease concept is the counter-balance to stigma as it serves to humanize, de-mystify, enlighten and objectify. Loss of control, impaired judgment, less than desirable behavior, destructive behavior, relationship breakdowns, unemployment, bankruptcy can be understood to be natural consequences of the disease. It makes it easier to respond compassionately. There is a consensus that the addict shouldn't be shamed because s/he is sick, nor because s/he is human!

Daniel@RelationshipVision.com   Copyrighted Materials 2007

References

<u>Night, Mother</u>, Marsha Norman

<u>Shame, The Power of Caring</u>, Gershen Kaufman

<u>Stigma</u>, Irving Goffman

www.ingramcontent.com/pod-product-compliance
Lightning Source LLC
Chambersburg PA
CBHW061951280526
45787CB00004B/1809